The Khmer Rouge: The Notorious History and Regime that Ruled Cambodia in the 1970s

By Charles River Editors

About Charles River Editors

Charles River Editors is a boutique digital publishing company, specializing in bringing history back to life with educational and engaging books on a wide range of topics. Keep up to date with our new and free offerings with this 5 2nd sign up on our weekly mailing list, and visit Our Kindle Author Page to see other recently published Kindle titles.

We make these books for you and always want to know our readers' opinions, so we encourage you to leave reviews and look forward to publishing new and exciting titles each week.

Introduction

Cambodian leader Pol Pot with Romanian leader Nicolae Ceauşescu

The Khmer Rouge

The reign of the Khmer Rouge, a Cambodian communist regime, began on April 7, 1975 as Khmer Rouge militants entered the Cambodian capital of Phnom Penh, ultimately gaining control and forcing out its residents. For the next four years, the regime would remain in power and commit what is now referred to as the Cambodian Genocide. Their reign would result in economic turmoil, cultural destruction, and mass death, impacting Cambodia to this day. That legacy continues to be the subject of discussion among governments and academics, who would debate not only their intentions and actions, but also the appropriate course of pursuing legal action against its leaders.

The Communist Party of Kampuchea, also known as the Khmer Rouge, took control of Cambodia's capital city of Phnom Penh on April 7, 1975. Upon seizing Phnom Penh, the communist forces of the Khmer Rouge began to eliminate all aspects of public life that were viewed as contrary to communist ideals. Military forces began to seize all private property, outlawed religion, repealed all existing laws, eliminated markets and currency, closed public gathering spaces, and declared all anti-regime activity as treason.

The existing borders of Cambodia, then known as Democratic Kampuchea, were immediately closed by the military. International citizens were not permitted to enter Cambodia and, more importantly, Cambodians were not permitted to exit. Citizens of all large cities, such as the capital of Phnom Penh, were quickly moved to the countryside to work in forced labor camps.

The ultimate goal of the Khmer Rouge regime was to return Cambodia to a nation centered around agriculture that lacked social classes and individuality. As a result, Pol Pot aimed to eliminate any groups he viewed as a barrier to achieving that vision, which mostly included ethnic, religious, and political groups within Cambodia. These groups ranged from Buddhist Monks and Muslim Cham to ethnic Thais and Vietnamese. Ethnic Khmer were also targeted, mainly for perceived political beliefs or activities. Over the course of about four years, millions of Cambodians would die at the hands of the Khmer Rouge regime. In all, the rise of the Khmer Rouge to power resulted in the deaths of over a million Cambodian residents and the diaspora of about 1.5 million Cambodians between 1975 and 1979. It would come to be known as the Cambodian Genocide.

The Khmer Rouge: The Notorious History and Legacy of the Communist Regime that Ruled Cambodia in the 1970s chronicles the destructive history of the regime and their impact on the region. Along with pictures depicting important people, places, and events, you will learn about the Khmer Rouge like never before.

The Khmer Rouge: The Notorious History and Legacy of the Communist Regime that Ruled Cambodia in the 1970s

About Charles River Editors

Introduction

The Founding of Cambodia

French Indochina

The Origins of the Khmer Rouge

The Vietnam War

The Khmer Rouge in Power

The End of the Khmer Rouge

Online Resources

Further Reading

Free Books by Charles River Editors

Discounted Books by Charles River Editors

The Founding of Cambodia

The Khmer Empire is best known for its large monuments, and other ancient sites from this empire still dot Cambodia's landscape due in large measure to the character of the land itself. For example, one common relic of the empire is the use of reservoirs, which remains an essential part of everyday life in Cambodia. The importance of these reservoirs largely has to do with Cambodia's geography, as it is dominantly a giant, flat plain with low mountain ranges (Cardamom Hills to the west and the Dangrek Mountains to the east). Running from north to south is the Mekong River, which flows slightly westward through Phnom Penh, Cambodia's modern-day capital. From there, it continues south toward Vietnam and branches out across the flat plains into numerous smaller streams, and from there it runs into the South China Sea. This river is roughly 4,200 kilometers long and is the fourth largest river (in terms of volume of flow) in Asia, beginning in Tibet (Zéphir 1998: 15). The Kulen Mountain region is near Angkor, considered the ancient capital of the Khmer Empire, but for the most part, the landscape is flat with the occasional hill, known as *phnoms*. These would play a significant role in the Khmer Empire's history, as they helped determine where rulers would establish their mortuary temples. The ancient belief in sacred hills is still alive today since almost every *phnom* is capped with a sacred Buddhist pagoda. These modern religious sites tend to be built on or very near ancient Khmer sites that were mostly dedicated to Hindu gods.

Cambodia's climate is affected by monsoons that result in dry and wet seasons. From around November-May, the climate is generally dry with high temperatures, which makes life difficult, especially from March-April. It is this seasonal drought period that made the construction of reservoirs a priority for any ruler, and this dependence on the water contributed to the development of sacred beliefs and mythology surrounding the water. If the seasonal cycle continues, the rainy season begins around June and lasts through October. These periods bring particularly heavy rain during the end of the season.

The heavy rainfall during the wet season has an enormous effect on the great lake known as Tonlé Sap, located in the middle of the vast plains. From June on, the lake rises, resulting in it almost quadrupling in size by the end of the rainy season. The monsoons are so powerful and the flow of the water is so strong that the Tonlé Sap River, flowing from Tonlé Sap to Phnom Penh and the Mekong, actually reverses its flow for a time due to the excessive flow of water. It also provides an ideal breeding ground for freshwater fish. The Tonlé Sap is, in fact, one of the largest sources of freshwater fish in Southeast Asia, even today, and it is likely that these waters played a significant role in the establishment of Angkor on the northern bank, just beyond the reach of high flood waters.

Fresh water is necessary for human survival in any part of the world, not only for quenching thirst but as a source of food and irrigation. Such a dependence on water and the dangerous droughts during the dry season led to the development of supernatural beliefs surrounding the life-giving waters. In the days before the Khmer Empire, the waters were symbolized by a mythical snake known as a *naga,* a multi-headed cobra associated with water and the benefits it provided, such as wealth through abundant crops.

The founding of Cambodia is even associated with a mythical serpent. The myth states that a Brahman of India named Kaundinya married the local snake-princess, named Soma. From this marriage, the first ancient royal lineage of Cambodia, the monarchs of Funan, a predecessor state to the Khmer Empire, was formed. It is possible this symbolic meeting between a foreign Indian priest and a local "snake" princess is based in some truth, such as the marriage of a foreign Indian priest or royalty to a local princess of people associated with sacred waters. The influence of Indian civilization on local populations, as will be discussed below, had a significant effect on the development of early civilizations of Cambodia and the Khmer.

Before the first civilizations had developed, beginning in the 1st or 2nd century CE, the people who entered Southeast Asia likely followed sources of freshwater from the north to the south. This much is linguistically supported by philologists linking the pre-Khmer people to the Yangzi Valley near Tibet. By 500 BCE, the pre-civilization inhabitants had become skilled bronze-workers and iron-workers. One tradition coming with these early inhabitants was the cultivation of rice. Once the monsoonal seasons were understood and local farmers were able to develop irrigation systems for farming rice, population sizes grew with the surplus of food. Larger populations that grew beyond extended families typically required an authority figure to maintain control through the establishment of rules or laws.

Since there are virtually no written records of or by the people during this period, it is difficult to understand what or how this authoritative rule may have been practiced. If the mythological founding of Funan has any truth behind it, it is possible that local city-states were ruled by regional royal families. What is understood of this time is that civilizations did not begin to develop until trade with India became commonplace and local rulers took advantage of city-states located near beneficial, navigational waters. Local ruling powers had control over what could be deemed large regions, but they were generally ruled from a fortified city.

By the 2nd century CE, India had firmly established trade contacts with Southeast Asia. The visitors from India were not interested in establishing colonies in Southeast Asia, but in obtaining the wealth they believed located there. Nonetheless, the pre-Khmer people were influenced to adopt numerous Indian traditions, in a process known as Indianization, which would result in numerous ideas and traditions becoming part of Khmer culture (Deedrick 2002). As more and more Indians established trading routes in and through Cambodia (to reach China), it is possible that traders and locals found it more beneficial to adopt the customs of these foreign traders. While the traders likely spread their beliefs to the willing locals, priests and gurus from India also traveled to Cambodia where they could teach Indian religions, scripts, and laws. It was through this contact that the holy script—known as Sanskrit—was adopted. Sanskrit's influence would have a lasting effect on local rulers and would be used by the Khmer rulers much later for inscriptions on monuments and buildings.

The first reports of the Funan came to European knowledge from the works of Paul Pelliot in 1903 when he began translating 3rd century CE Chinese reports of maritime trade, recorded by Kang Dai and Zhu Ying, envoys of the Wu emperor. According to his translations of the Dai and Ying texts, there were walled settlements and palaces for various rulers who had enacted a system of taxation to collect gold, silver, perfumes, and pearls. The kingdom itself is described as "more than 3000 li [one li equals 540 meters] west of Linyi [also known as Champa situated in central and southern Vietnam] in a large bay of the sea...There are walled towns, palaces and dwelling houses. The men...practice farming...They like to engrave ornaments and to carve...They have books and keep archives...The characters of their writing resemble those of the Hou [a people from central Asia with writing developed from Indian characters]." (Higham 2013: 101-102).

As the ancient and medieval history suggests, the geographical position of Cambodia has left it the subject of consistent disputes. In the modern age, Thailand and Vietnam historically struggled for domination over the region separating their respective nations. The earliest sign of Thai and Vietnamese interference in Cambodia can be traced to the mid-18th century, at which point Cambodia became a protectorate of both Vietnam and Thailand, ultimately ceding territory to its neighbors and experiencing widespread political turmoil.

Cambodia regularly made financial tributes and ceded land to both Vietnam and Thailand between the mid-18th century and the 1820s. However, the Vietnamese successfully drove the Thai out of Cambodia in 1833, obtaining all Thai-possessed Cambodian land in the process. From this point forward, Cambodian would solely be a protectorate of Vietnam.

At this point, the Vietnamese would attempt to implement their ideals throughout Cambodia, primarily in terms of culture. The people of Cambodia were resistant to turn from their cultural traditions and overall way of life, leading to a variety of revolts against Vietnam's occupation of the region. By the 1840s—only ten years after the Vietnamese had seized control of Cambodia—these revolts were strong enough to topple Vietnamese rule.

Thailand saw this as an opportunity to once again gain power of Cambodia, establishing itself as a stronger opponent of its rival, Vietnam. After Thai forces moved into Cambodia, the Vietnamese re-entered the region to protect their interest and prevent Thai forces from gaining wider access to Vietnamese borders. This resulted in warfare that ultimately ended with a peace negotiation between the nations of Cambodia, Thailand, and Vietnam in 1846.

The 1846 peace negotiation aimed to establish Cambodia as an independent nation, serving as a buffer state between the powerful states of Thailand and Vietnam. The two nations accepted that neither could exert control over Cambodia and maintain peace, thereby necessitating

Cambodia as an independent power. This agreement resulted in both Thai and Vietnamese forces withdrawing from Cambodia, recognizing Ang Duong as Cambodia's king.

These negotiations, however, did not account for the growing European interest in Indochina, particularly when it came to the French.

French Indochina

Beginning in the 14th and 15th centuries, the vast majority of Asia was a source of wonderment to European explorers, full of potential adrenaline and mystery. Explorations that ventured into the region were few and far between, and the stories that returned were often romanticized with tales of mysterious people and creatures. Despite regular trade with the modern-day Middle East, Asia was relatively untouched. For the most part, Catholic missionaries held the primary interest for exploring the region, as they hoped to spread Christianity prior to the influence of other cultures on Asia[1].

Prior to the Europeans' arrival in Indochina, the region had relatively little infrastructure. Its sole economic pursuit was agriculture, and agricultural practices, in many ways, were simply a means of sustenance. While minor trade occurred, the majority of production remained within Indochina. Furthermore, the region only had one main road, known as the Mandarin Road, which was essentially a dirt track spanning both vast plains and rugged mountain terrain. Aside from this road, the locals relied on narrow, overgrown paths and bamboo bridges. There was no mail service, and no centralized government services.

Thus, despite their early interest, European missionaries did not regularly make their way into Asia until the late 16th and early 17th centuries. While still motivated to spread Christianity to the region prior to the introduction of outside influences, the Church was now motivated to expand due to the effects of the Reformation. The Catholic establishment had lost a significant amount of prestige and, in turn, needed to reestablish the power it once had. As a result, it funded regular mission trips into the region. However, the missionaries were soon pushed out of the "Far East" (modern day China) by the Japanese, who forced the missionaries to recede into Indochina (parts of modern day Cambodia, Laos, and Vietnam).

Now based in Indochina, the missionaries had mixed success converting locals to Christianity. Historically, the region was under strong Chinese influence resulting in Buddhism, Taoism, and Confucianism taking hold. Regardless of their success—or lack thereof—in converting locals, the missionaries were successful in implementing other changes. The locals had developed a language based on Chinese characters, but they desired to separate themselves from the oligarchical government implemented by China. As a result, they readily adopted the Latin characters introduced by missionaries, adding accents to create what is now recognized as the modern "quoc ngu" alphabet (essentially Latin characters with unique, phonetic accents)[2].

---

[1] Ennis T, French Policy and Developments in Indochina (Chicago: The University of Chicago Press, 1936), 13

Despite the efforts of early missionaries and the acceptance of the newly introduced alphabet, European influence was not widely appreciated in Indochina. Local leaders were afraid that the presence of missionaries would encourage international trade. This trade, in turn, could encourage European political influence. As a result, the emperor banned all missionaries and western influencers from the region. However, a ban of this nature is nearly impossible to enforce. In practice, it prevented formal recognition of western powers but still allowed missionaries to continue entering the region.

However, anti-Western sentiments were not equally applied to all European countries. France, in particular, made significant diplomatic gains within Indochina. King Louis XIV went as far as to secure a truce between the government of Indochina and French missionaries, allowing their continued presence.[3]

King Louis XIV

As the French learned more about what Indochina had to offer both materially and financially, the region became of even greater interest for colonization. As a result, the French entered the mid-18th century with the goal of further exploring and settling vast swaths of the region. Most

---

[2] Lach D, Asia in the Making of Europe: The Century of Discovery, vol. I, book II (Chicago: The University of Chicago Press, 1965), 560
[3] Ennis, French Policy and Developments in Indochina, 5, 22-2

notable during this time period are the travels of Pierre Poivre, who provided economic insight that informed French ventures throughout the region. In 1747, Poivre worked alongside the French East India Company to establish commercial relationships with locals throughout Indochina, but this effort was a failure due to a lack of Indochinese interest in Western products. This came as a severe blow to France, which hoped to establish a stronghold in Southeast Asia to make up for their territorial losses to Great Britain in the Seven Years' War (which included parts of modern Canada and all North American land east of the Mississippi river).[4]

Poivre

In order to secure their interests moving into the 19th century, the French began to more directly interfere in Indochinese politics. In the 1770s, Emperor Gia Long, known as Emperor Nguyen Anh at the time, was expelled from his throne. Emperor Anh then appealed to the French government for aid and ultimately fled to France to reside with a Bishop. In 1801, the French government offered Emperor Anh military assistance to reclaim the throne, and in return for their

---

[4] Roberts S, The History of French Colonial Policy (1870-1925), vol. II, 422

support, the emperor created open trade borders for the French and entered a treaty of friendship. As a result of his support, the French would continue to strengthen both their trade relations and base in Indochina over the next 20 years.

Emperor Gia Long

Despite their interference, the French would not remain on good terms with the leader of Indochina. Upon Emperor Gia Long's departure from the throne, his son, Emperor Minh-Mang, rose to power. Emperor Minh-Mang held anti-Western views and demanded that all foreigners, including the French who had long enjoyed special privileges, leave the region. When the French refused due to their economic holdings, the emperor responded by persecuting Christian missionaries in the region.[5]

---

[5] Stern, The French Colonies, 192

Emperor Minh-Mang

Contemporary depictions of Christians being executed

While anti-Western sentiments persisted among subsequent emperors, the French would soon benefit from a significant turning point. In 1847, Emperor Tu-Duc rose to power. Much like his grandfather, Emperor Minh-Mang, he held anti-Western sentiments, and when the Revolution of 1848 took place in France, he seized what he perceived as an opportunity to rid Indochina of Christian missionaries altogether. Persecution heightened, and Emperor Tu-Duc refused to negotiate with Napoleon III. As a result, the French entered Indochina by force with claims that missionaries were in physical danger and that the French ruler had been insulted.[6]

---

[6] Ennis, French Policy and Development, 33-35

Emperor Tu-Duc

Throughout the next decade, the French would continue to dispatch warships to Indochina, claiming that they were seeking to protect missionaries, and eventually, the French would come to occupy a variety of coastal towns. In an effort to save his empire, Emperor Tu-Duc eventually entered the Treaty of Saigon in 1862, turning over three provinces of eastern Indochina to the French (what is now western Cambodia, western Laos, and eastern Vietnam) and two island provinces.[7]

Now that they had control over significant portions of Indochina, the French opened large portions of the region to both trade and military movement, but while exploring the Red River for potential trade opportunities, French colonists began to experience a variety of complications. Since France only occupied eastern Indochina, rebel forces relied on western regions to launch attacks on French settlements, so in an effort to protect their economic interests, the French decided to invade Indochina's western provinces as well. This invasion began in 1867, and by 1869 the French had gained full control of the Mekong River Delta[8].

In 1863, French forces officially formed colonies throughout Indochina, particularly in portions of modern-day Vietnam and Cambodia, less than 20 years after Ang Duong was made king of an

---

[7] Ennis, French Policy and Development, 41
[8] Roberts, The History of French Colonial Policy, vol. II, 422-423

independent Cambodia. The individual colonies were spread out, relatively weak, and dealing with populations that were becoming more and more hostile, and as a whole, France was losing control of its Indochinese colonies.

Fortunately for the French, the tide would turn in 1873 with the French capture of Hanoi and the Red River Delta. This success would lead to the signing of the Franco-Annamite Treaty in 1874, forcing the emperor to officially recognize French claims to Indochinese land.[9]

Of course, this did not equate to the end of land disputes in Indochina. The Chinese government continuously protested the involvement of the French in Indochina, especially as the French went on to create multiple protectorates in the region. In 1883, the French entered the Treaty of Hué with Annam (modern central Vietnam) and Tonkin (modern Red River Delta), which established both Tonkin and Cambodia as French protectorates. This gave the French full rights to interfere in political affairs throughout Annam, Tonkin, and Cambodia.

---

[9] Power T, Jules Ferry and the Renaissance of French Imperialism, 156

A French marine in Tonkin in the 1880s

Ultimately, China refused to accept the validity of the Treaty of Hué, and in turn, Chinese troops were sent into the Tonkin region to eliminate French influence. In hopes of alleviating the fighting, France reached out to Great Britain to resolve the issue, and the British offered to enforce a neutral zone between China and Tonkin, but the Chinese refused and demanded that France recognize their sovereignty in Annam[10]. The sides would eventually reach a settlement in 1884 with the Treaty of Tien-Tsin, which required the Chinese to leave Tonkin and called on the French to acknowledge the Chinese border. Furthermore, it ensured free trade between China and the Annam region. Misunderstanding led to further disputes, but the Chinese would eventually recognize the Treaty of Hué and reach a peace settlement.

---

[10] Power T, Jules Ferry and the Renaissance of French Imperialism, 160

Meanwhile, Ang Duong, the king since 1846, died in 1860, and his successor, Norodom, served as Cambodia's acting leader. Throughout his early rule, Norodom was amiable with the French, going as far as to accept French gifts and enter an agreement establishing Cambodia as a French tributary state. When Norodom visited Thailand to be officially crowned king, the French moved in and established Cambodia's capital as a French possession. Upon Norodom's return, the French ultimately exited the Cambodian capital and returned it to Cambodian control.

However, Cambodian independence from France would not last. Despite an initial acceptance of France's interference in Cambodia, the region's leaders eventually came to resist French reformation efforts, while the French aimed to establish cultural influence in Cambodia as they had in Vietnam several decades prior. Resistance proved relatively futile in light of French military superiority and its stronghold of Vietnam. By the 1860s, France would control Cambodia, and the French would maintain that control through the 1930s.

By the turn of the 20th century, the works of French philosophers and political documents such as America's Declaration of Independence made their way to the Indochinese elites via Chinese translations. Eventually, the work of Karl Marx, H.G. Wells, and Charles Darwin would reach Indochinese shores, exposing the elite to a diverse array of ideology. As a result, the elite intellectual class of the 1920s and 1930s became extremely interested in global affairs, and this rise of intellectualism among the Indochinese elite allowed a new rebel group, known as the "new intelligentsia," to gain prominence. Members of this group were generally intellectuals who were concerned with both liberal thought and the cultural history of Indochina. A revival took place which honored and idolized Indochinese historical figures who resisted against the Chinese occupation of the region. The group agreed that returning to pre-colonial Indochina was impossible, but they recognized the need for change. And the general populace, having suffered under French rule for decades, sympathized with their cause.

Initially, these rebels and intellectuals staged ineffective rebellions. They failed to unify, and this resulted in small-scale rebellions that could be easily halted and dismissed by French officials. This pattern of small-scale rebellions being squashed by French forces would continue until Ho Chi Minh gained prominence in the 1920s. As a rebel leader, he mobilized Indochinese students into a group referred to as the Revolutionary Youth League, and this group, though large in scale, organized into small cells in an attempt to avoid the attention of French forces.[11]

---

[11] Marr D, Vietnamese Tradition on Trial, 1920-1945 (Berkeley: University of California Press, 1981).

Ho Chi Minh

The Great Depression proved to be the perfect time for Ho Chi Minh to strike. Rice and rubber prices had dropped, cutting both production and wages, leading to workers across the nation going on strike. Ho Chi Minh rallied the proletariat, directing their anger at the French colonizers, and he managed to unify the three rival Communist factions within Indochina to form the Indochinese Communist Party, which ultimately called for independence from France and for the rise of the proletariat into positions of power.

The struggle for independence went on, but everything took a backseat when World War II started. As France faced Nazi occupation in Europe, the Japanese made their way through Asia, and they would conquer Indochina, pushing the French out before moving on to push the British out of Malaysia. The Japanese also ejected the Dutch from Indonesia and the Americans from the Philippines. Their final push removed European influence from Southeast Asia altogether, allowing Ho Chi Minh's group of rebels to seize full control of Indochina and bringing the communist regime to power.

France had lost control of the region during the war, and the Japanese encouraged the nations formerly colonized by France to pursue total independence. In 1945, the Japanese would grant the nation of Cambodia full independence, but the French would return just one year later in 1946. Cambodian leaders would sign an agreement with France allowing Cambodia to form its own constitution and political factions so long as it remained a French protectorate. This agreement allowed Cambodians the political independence they desired, as well as the backing of a powerful country which could, theoretically, defend their interests in times of war.

Out of this agreement, the Communist Party of Kampuchea was born. It was headed by Cambodians who spoke Vietnamese, eventually bringing in Pol Pot, the future leader of the Khmer Rouge, and his supporters. For the most part, the Communist Party of Kampuchea was supported by young Cambodians. The vast majority were socioeconomically advantaged, having studied in France as children. During their time in France, many of the Communist Party of Kampuchea's early supporters held radical ideas, bringing them back to Cambodia and becoming known as Cambodia's "radical generation."

By 1953, the Communist Party of Kampuchea was growing stronger and stronger. More and more affluent, young Cambodians were returning from France and radicalizing the nation's political sphere. And with the First Indochina War taking place in neighboring Vietnam, France's resources were spread too thin to deny Cambodian requests for independence. Faced with seemingly endless Cambodian resistance, the French eventually agreed later in 1953 to grant Cambodia independence, allowing King Sihanouk full control over the nation's military, judicial system, and foreign relations.

Even as the French maintained influence in Cambodia, it was slipping away in Vietnam. When the Japanese surrendered and relinquished all claim to its overseas empire, spontaneous uprisings occurred in Hanoi, Hue, and other Vietnamese cities. These were seized upon by the Vietnam Independence League (or *Vietminh*) and Ho Chi Minh, who declared an independent Democratic Republic of Vietnam (DRV) on September 2, 1945.

France, which had reoccupied most of the country by early 1946, agreed in theory to grant the DRV limited autonomy. However, when the sharp limits of that autonomy became apparent, the Vietminh took up arms. By the end of 1946, in the first instance of what would become a longstanding pattern, the French managed to retain control of the cities while the rebels held sway in the countryside. From the outset, Ho hoped to avoid conflict with the United States. He was a deeply committed Communist and dedicated to class warfare and social revolution, but at the same time, he was also a steadfast Vietnamese nationalist who remained wary of becoming a puppet of the Soviet Union or the People's Republic of China. Indeed, Ho's very real popularity throughout the country rested to no small extent on his ability to tap into a centuries-old popular tradition of national resistance against powerful foreign occupiers, a tradition originally directed against imperial China. As such, he made early advances to Washington, even deliberately echoing the American Declaration of Independence in his own declaration of Vietnamese independence. Under different circumstances, Americans might not have objected much to a communist but independent DRV. The Roosevelt and Truman administrations had trumpeted national independence in Asia and exhibited almost nothing but contempt for French colonial rule. However, as Cold War tensions rose, and as the Soviet Union and (after 1949) Communist

China increased their material and rhetorical support for the Vietminh cause, such subtle gradations quickly faded. Considering the matter in May 1949, Secretary of State Dean Acheson asserted that the question of whether Ho was "as much nationalist as Commie is irrelevant. All Stalinists in colonial areas are nationalists . . . Once in power their objective necessarily becomes subordination [of the] state to Commie purpose." (Young, 20 – 23).

In 1951, while war was raging in Korea, the United States began signing defense pacts with nations in the Pacific, forging alliances in an attempt to prevent Communism from spreading. As the Korean War was coming to an end, the nation joined the Southeast Asia Treaty Organization, thereby promising to defend several nations in the area from Communist aggression. One of those nations was the tiny country of South Vietnam.

As a result, the United States recognized the new puppet government France had established under the emperor Bao Dai, and by 1953 American financial aid funded fully 60% of France's counterinsurgency effort. When that effort finally collapsed in 1954, an international conference at Geneva agreed to divide Vietnam at the 17th parallel into a communist DRV in the north and an American-backed Republic of Vietnam in the south. Between 1955 and 1961, South Vietnam and its new president, Ngo Dinh Diem, received more than $1 billion in American aid. Even so, Diem proved unable to consolidate support for his regime, and by 1961 he faced a growing insurgency in the Viet Cong, a coalition of local guerrilla groups supported and directed by North Vietnam.

Diem

Bao Dai

As Diem and his successors teetered on the brink of disaster, American politicians and military officers grappled with the difficult question of how much they were willing to sacrifice to support an ally. In 1961, President Kennedy resisted a push to mount air strikes, but he agreed to send increased financial aid to South Vietnam, along with hundreds (and eventually thousands) of American "military advisors." With that, the stage was set for the Vietnam War

Cambodia's independence from France would be solidified in 1954 when the French lost their hold on Vietnam. France lacked the resources to continue fighting in Indochina, and was eventually forced to sign the Geneva Agreement, which required France to end any involvement in Southeast Asia, including their political interference in Cambodia.

Of course, French influence was not the only factor influencing Cambodian politics during this period. The United States and the North Vietnamese would engage in hostilities as the Americans aimed to prevent the spread of communism from Mao Zedong's regime in China throughout Asia. American strategists associated Vietnam's communists with China's communists, ultimately aiming to eradicate their influence within Indochina.

The Origins of the Khmer Rouge

The fighting throughout Southeast Asia in the first half of the 20th century emboldened Cambodian communists, especially the man who would lead the Khmer Rouge. Similar to many of his contemporaries, Pol Pot came from an affluent background, having begun his education at a private school in Phnom Penh before transferring to France and learning about communist history throughout the world. In fact, some evidence points to Pol Pot joining the French Communist Party in 1952 prior to returning to Cambodia. This clearly demonstrates the French influence on Pol Pot's political views, but he would also go on to take ideas from Mao Zedong, the communist leader of neighboring China who would become a close friend and confidant.

Mao's philosophy on class struggle, eliminating political opponents, and political revolution both interested and inspired Pol Pot. Upon returning to Cambodia, he would work to implement a similar type of revolution, stomping out any opposition and creating a society he believed would be free of class struggle In 1963, Pol Pot's path to revolution began when he became the secretary of the Communist Party of Kampuchea, and he would remain secretary until the April 1975 takeover of Phnom Penh, establishing the Khmer Rouge regime.

Mao

Naturally, Pol Pot was also influenced by Ho Chi Minh, who formed the Communist Party of Vietnam in 1930 when he championed the unification of individual communist groups that developed throughout Vietnam in the 1920s. In an effort to expand its reach, the Communist Party of Vietnam was soon coined the Indochinese Communist Party in an effort to attract both Cambodian and Laos communists. However, this effort did not prove effective, with the vast majority of its members consisting of Vietnamese individuals. Although some Cambodians would go on to join the Indochinese Communist Party following the Second World War, its overall impact on Cambodian politics was shadowed by the influence of the Kampuchea People's Revolutionary Party.

Following the Second World War, Vietnamese and Thai leftists would continue to put pressure on Cambodians to not only struggle for independence from the French, but to adopt communist ideals. During their fight against French forces in the First Indochina War, communist Vietnamese forces regularly entered Cambodia and eventually aided in the formation of a militant, leftist Cambodian force that would come to be known as the Khmer Issarak. In April 1950, the Khmer Issarak would establish the United Issarak Front, led by Son Ngoc Minh with a significant portion of its leadership consisting of Indochinese Communist Party members. It would go on to hold roughly a sixth of Cambodia's territory by 1952 and roughly half of the country's territory by 1954.

However, the Indochinese Communist Party was not around to stay. In 1951, the party was officially disbanded and broke into the Vietnam Workers' party, Laos Issara, and Kampuchean People's Revolutionary Party. From this point forward, Cambodia's communist movement would grow independent of its neighboring countries, although it is important to note that the leaders of the Kampuchean People's Revolutionary Party tended to be ethnic Cambodians raised in Vietnam and ethnic Vietnamese living in Cambodia. Individuals lacking foreign influence of some sort were relatively uninvolved in the inner workings and strategic planning of the Kampuchean People's Revolutionary Party as a whole.

Initially, the Kampuchean People's Revolutionary Party failed to gain the traction it needed to effectively implement a communist regime within Cambodia. During the Geneva Conference of 1954, the Vietnamese did not secure a formula political role for the Kampuchean People's Revolutionary Party moving forward. In response, roughly 1,000 Cambodians associated with the Kampuchean People's Revolutionary Party entered North Vietnam and lived in a state of exile. Members of the Kampuchean People's Revolutionary Party who did not leave Cambodia went on to form the Pracheachon Party, the legal political face of the Kampuchean People's Revolutionary Party. This "new" party participated in the 1955 and 1958 elections, but failed to garner enough votes to hold legislative seats.

Following these defeats, individuals associated with the Pracheachon Party were the subject of much ridicule and harassment within the Cambodian political sphere as they did not work alongside Cambodia's existing leadership, known as Sangkum and headed by King Siahnouk. As a result, its membership was barred from participating in the 1962 Cambodian elections and eventually went underground. Throughout this time, King Sihanouk referred to the group as the Khmer Rouge, which is the name it would adopt upon implementing the communist regime headed by Pol Pot in 1975.

While struggling to find its place in Cambodian politics, the Kampuchea People's Revolutionary Party split into two distinct factions: the urban and rural committees. While complex in nature, the urban committee was backed by Vietnamese communists and generally believed that the Sihanouk government could be worked with, as King Sihanouk was relatively neutral, distrustful of the United States, and had secured Cambodian independence from France. The urban committee believed that Sihanouk could persuaded to adopt leftist policies over time. On the other hand, the rural committee believed that urban elites were out of touch with the realities of Cambodian life, and that the government should be immediately overthrown to alleviate the suffering resulting from perceived class struggle and the feudalist policies of the Sihanouk government.

King Sihanouk

Throughout the period of French colonization, affluent Cambodian families would send their children to France to receive a formal education. During the 1950s, Cambodian students studying in Paris would organize a small-scale communist movement primarily independent from the communist movements occurring simultaneously in Cambodia and Indochina as a whole. These students, upon returning to Cambodia, would take over the party infrastructure throughout the 1960s. Ultimately, these members of what came to be known as the Paris Student Group would lead an insurgent movement that established the Khmer Rouge regime in April 1975 and toppled the existing communist party.

Alongside Pol Pot, who had studied in Paris on the way to becoming fixated with classical French literature and the political and economic theories of Karl Marx, Ieng Sary, a student of Chinese and Khmer descent who was raised in Vietnam, would also come to take on a prominent role in the Paris Student Group. Born in 1925, Ieng Sary studied in a Phnom Penh high school prior to pursuing a degree at a Parisian university of economics and politics in the 1950s. He was closely associated with both Hou Yuon and Son Sen, who also played primary roles in the Paris Student Group. These two students, slightly younger than Ieng Sary and Pol Pot, studied education, literature, and law in Paris, ultimately earning doctorate degrees in their respective fields.

Ieng Sary

Of all of the students associated with the Paris Student Group, the vast majority came from landowner and civil servant backgrounds. In fact, Pol Pot and Hou Yuon are believed to have had blood connections to the royal family itself. Furthermore, Pol Pot's older sister served as a concubine of a former king, and both Pol Pot and Long Sary married women who were potentially related to the royal family. Thus, despite holding views that glorified agrarian life, the members of the Paris Student Group were members of the upper-class themselves.

As a group, the members of the Paris Student Group also developed relatively similar political views. A significant portion of the Cambodian students staying in Paris adopted the tenets of Marxism-Leninism early on in their studies. Furthermore, various members, including both Pol Pot and Ieng Sary, joined the French Communist Party in the early 1950s. This political awakening is considered to be one of the primary reasons the Khmer Rouge came to exist. Having met ethnic Cambodians who fought alongside Vietnamese communist forces, the Paris Student Group came to believe that Cambodian communists were far too subservient to their

Vietnamese counterparts, and that an armed revolution was needed to truly establish Cambodia as a classless, communist state.

With that in mind, the Paris Student Group reorganized the Parisian Khmer Students Association, which had a membership of roughly two-hundred Cambodians, into a think tank for nationalist, leftist ideas. The recognized Khmer Student Association and its successors included a secret organization aimed at inciting a communist revolution in Cambodia. This group was known as the Marxist Circle and its most notable members were Pol Pot, Hou Youn, and Long Sary. In 1952, the secret organization penned a letter to King Sihanouk, the ruler of Cambodia at the time, and referred to him as a barrier to democracy. French authorities would go on to bar the group from meeting, but Hou Young went on to establish a new group, the Khmer Students Union, which continued the work of the Marxist Circle.

Aside from direct political action, the academic work of the Paris Student Group would prove significant in the development of the Khmer Rouge and its guiding principles. Hou Yuon and Khieu Samphan, both having written doctoral papers in Paris, focused on political and economic themes that would become the centerpiece of Khmer Rouge policy. Hou Youn focused on the social and political role of peasant farmers in Cambodian development, ultimately negating the widespread opinion that urbanization is a required step of national development. Khieu Samphan wrote a later doctoral paper that argued Cambodia must become independent of its neighbors and entirely self-reliant in terms of all resources to truly achieve a just society, ultimately arguing that Western nations had crippled Cambodia via economic domination that prohibited true development within the country.

Pol Pot returned to Cambodia from his studies in Paris in 1953, along with many other members of the notorious Paris Student Group, and became immediately involved in the the Kampuchean People's Revolutionary Party. His first venture into Cambodian communist circles was to fight alongside Vietnamese forces in rural Cambodian communities. Following the fighting against the French, Pol Pot would return to the capital city of Phnom Penh, where he worked closely with the communist party, ultimately serving as the liaison between the visible leftist parties and the hidden, more radical communist movement in Cambodia.

Pol Pot's Parisian contemporaries, however, would not take on such active roles in the Cambodian political sphere. Ieng Sary and Hou Yuon both became instructors at a newly constructed private school in Phnom Penh, which was founded with the help of Hou Yuon particularly. Similarly, Khieu Samphan became a professor of law at the University of Phnom Penh, where he founded a leftist publication, *L'Observateur*, which became widespread among Cambodian academics. The publication held anti-establishment views, and as a result the royal police barred its production and ultimately beat, undressed, and photographed Khieu Samphan in public to make an example for other leftists who opposed the monarchy.

Nonetheless, Khieu Samphan went on to cooperate with Sihanouk, going as far as to urge his leftist counterparts to join forces with the monarchy in an effort to eliminate the presence of the United States in Vietnam. Eventually, Khieu Samphan, Hou Yuon, and Hu Nim would all join the royal government in official posts, granting them the access and insight the Khmer Rouge would need for its eventual overthrow of the monarchy.

Meanwhile, leftists who did not work directly with the royal government were devising plans of their own. In September 1960, leaders of the Kampuchean People's Revolutionary Party held a congress in secret, and though it is unclear what occurred during this meeting due to revisionism among Cambodia's communist factions, the general topic of discussion was whether the party should work alongside or fight against King Sihanouk and the royal government. In the end, the party would adopt an official stance of cooperation, reorganizing its leadership to reflect that shift in political procedure. Tou Samouth was named its general secretary, with Nuon Chex serving as deputy general security, and Pol Pot and Ieng Sary took on the third and fifth highest positions in the party, respectively.

The Kampuchean People's Revolutionary Party also rebranded itself as the Workers' Party of Kampuchea. This symbolically made it an equal of the Vietnam Workers' Party, which had long interfered with Cambodian politics, and established the group as an independent, Cambodian communist movement. As a result, the September 1960 meeting came to be known as the Second Congress of the Kampuchean People's Revolutionary Party rather than the First Congress of the Workers' Party of Kampuchea.

Less than two years after the creation of the Workers' Party of Kampuchea, its leader, Tou Samouth, was assassinated by the royal government, and the following year, 1963, Pol Pot was elected as the new leader of the party. At this point, Pol Pot removed Tou Samouth's allies from power, as he considered them too in favor of Vietnamese influence. He took the same approach to other members of the party, ultimately filling the vast majority of party positions with members of the Paris Student Group and other likeminded leftists who desired an independent communist revolution in Cambodia.

In July 1963, the year of Pol Pot's rise to the head position of the Workers' Party of Kampuchea, he and the party's central leadership fled to an insurgent base in rural Cambodia. This was in response to King Sihanouk placing Pol Pot, Chou Chet, and a variety of other leftist leaders on a list to be summoned to the royal palace to declare their loyalty to the monarchy. Pol Pot and Chou Chet were the only two on the list to escape Phnom Penh, with the remaining leftists being forced to cooperate with King Sihanouk and being kept under constant police surveillance.

When Pol Pot and other leaders of the Workers' Party of Kampuchea fled to the insurgent base, it was in a region occupied by ethnic minorities known as the Khmer Loeu, who lived in small tribes and had historically experienced forced resettlement and assimilation at the hands of the monarchy. In Pol Pot's eyes, this made them excellent candidates for soldiers in a communist revolution against the existing government, but the party was not yet ready to mobilize those forces.

In order to prepare for an armed reovlution, Pol Pot first made visits to Northern Vietnam and China in 1965, receiving significant training and ensuring that the two groups would not aid the monarchy in the event of a dispute. The following year, the Workers' Party of Kampuchea was renamed the Communist Party of Kampuchea, though the change was not made known to the vast majority of the party since it implied a desire for armed revolution. Instead, the group maintained the front of a leftist organization that sought to exist alongside or in opposition to the government, rather than to replace the royal government itself.

Throughout 1967, the Communist Party of Kampuchea attempted arm struggle, but saw limited success in rising against Sihanouk. A year later, however, the tides changed, and the Khmer Rouge as it is now known was officially established. The group initiated armed revolution throughout the entirety of Cambodia to dismantle the monarchy, and the North Vietnamese, although not made aware in advance of the Khmer Rouge's plan to strike, supplied men, accommodations, and artillery to the Khmer Rouge to aid in their revolutionary efforts. Since Pol Pot had established the support of the North Vietnamese the prior year, the Khmer Rouge gained a competitive advantage that King Sihanouk's military could not compete with, and as the revolution grew in size, the party eventually announced that it was now known as the Communist Party of Kampuchea, rather than the Workers' Party of Kampuchea.

In addition to the ongoing armed efforts to topple the existing government, the Khmer Rouge gained traction due to political unrest within the Cambodian monarchy. King Sihanouk was removed as head of state in March 1970, exiled to China, and replaced by Premier Lon Nol. Somewhat remarkably, while in exile, King Sihanouk sought to ally with the Khmer Rouge, and with the support of China he established what was known as the Royal Government of the National Union of Kampuchea, which served as a government-in-exile. In contrast, Premier Lon Nol formed the Khmer Republic with the support of the United States, despite American fears of having to engage in armed combat due to Premier Lon Nol's weak military forces.

Lon Nol

Giving the increasing size of the revolution, the North Vietnamese government officially intervened in the war in March 1970 following the exile of King Sihanouk, sending forces to attack Premie Lon Nol's military. Future records would show that this was done at the request of Nuon Chea, a Khmer Rouge leader who had negotiated with North Vietnam to aid in the revolution. These North Vietnamese forces succeeded in taking large portions of Cambodia, nearly reaching the capital of Phnom Penh before retreating from the Cambodian Army. By June 1970, the North Vietnamese had taken roughly a third of Cambodia and handed it over to the Khmer Rouge. In addition, the Khmer Rouge independently captured large portions of southern Cambodia.

The support of former King Sihanouk proved extremely beneficial to the revolutionary efforts of the Khmer Rouge regime. The former king made a public show of supporting the Khmer Rouge directly on the battlefield, after which the Khmer Rouge army went from 6,000 volunteer fighters to roughly 50,000. The vast majority of these new supporters were not communists, but loyalists who supported the king and held no leftist political views. In fact, the people of Cambodia were so blindly supportive of former King Sihanouk that the Khmer Rouge was able to occupy a majority of Cambodia by 1973, employing de facto political and economic control over the country while the majority of Cambodians believed King Sihanouk would be restored to power following the defeat of Premier Lon Nol.

The Vietnam War

Before the Vietnam War, most Americans would have been hard pressed to locate Vietnam on a map. South Vietnamese President Diem's regime was extremely unpopular, and war broke out between North Vietnam and South Vietnam around the end of the 1950s. Kennedy's administration tried to prop up the South Vietnamese with training and assistance, but the South Vietnamese military was feeble. A month before his death, Kennedy signed a presidential directive withdrawing 1,000 American personnel, and shortly after Kennedy's assassination, new President Lyndon B. Johnson reversed course, instead opting to expand American assistance to South Vietnam.

Over the next few years, the American military commitment to South Vietnam grew dramatically, and the war effort became both deeper and more complex. The strategy included parallel efforts to strengthen the economic and political foundations of the South Vietnamese regime, to root out the Viet Cong guerrilla insurgency in the south, combat the more conventional North Vietnamese Army (NVA) near the Demilitarized Zone between north and south, and bomb military and industrial targets in North Vietnam itself. In public, American military officials and members of the Johnson administration stressed their tactical successes and offered rosy predictions; speaking before the National Press Club in November 1967, General Westmoreland claimed, "I have never been more encouraged in the four years that I have been in Vietnam. We are making real progress...I am absolutely certain that whereas in 1965 the enemy was winning, today he is certainly losing." (New York Times, November 22, 1967).

At the same time, the government worked to conceal from the American public their own doubts and the grim realities of war. Reflecting on the willful public optimism of American officials at the time, Colonel Harry G. Summers concluded, "We in the military knew better, but through fear of reinforcing the basic antimilitarism of the American people we tended to keep this knowledge to ourselves and downplayed battlefield realities...We had concealed from the American people the true nature of the war." (Summers, 63).

By the end of 1967, with nearly half a million troops deployed, more than 19,000 deaths, and a war that cost $2 billion a month and seemed to grow bloodier by the day, the Johnson administration faced an increasingly impatient and skeptical nation. Early in 1968, a massive coordinated Viet Cong operation - the Tet Offensive - briefly paralyzed American and South Vietnamese forces across the country, threatening even the American embassy compound in Saigon. With this, the smiling mask slipped even further, inflaming the burgeoning antiwar movement. Although American soldiers didn't lose a battle strategically during the campaign, the Tet Offensive made President Johnson non-credible and historically unpopular, to the extent that he did not run for reelection in 1968. By then, Vietnam had already fueled the hippie counterculture, and anti-war protests spread across the country. On campuses and in the streets, some protesters spread peace and love, but others rioted. In August 1968, riots broke out in the streets of Chicago, as the National Guard and police took on 10,000 anti-war rioters during the Democratic National Convention. By the end of the decade, Vietnam had left tens of thousands of Americans dead, spawned a counterculture with millions of protesters, and destroyed a presidency, and more was still yet to come.

As the results of the Tet Offensive made clear, American forces were hamstrung by political constraints and a wide range of self-imposed limitations, and the United States struggled to deal with the greater strategic nimbleness of the North Vietnamese during the late 1960s. The tremendous power of the American military, blending technological strength and professional skill, gave the Americans the advantage in many, though of course not all, tactical encounters. On the strategic and operational level, however, the North Vietnamese held many of the trump cards. Constrained by a heavily defensive strategy, the U.S. found itself mostly forced to respond to the North's initiatives, and a reactive strategy placed even an extremely potent combatant at a severe disadvantage.

The North Vietnamese, on the other hand, fought a war of conquest motivated by a form of imperialistic communism. After ruthlessly imposing their Marxist creed on the north's population and butchering those who resisted, Ho Chi Minh's cadres and their successors pursued victory against South Vietnam without qualms or restrictions. Though often outmatched on the battlefield by their American opponents, they pursued victory by any and all means, untroubled by the objections of conscience and unrestrained by the public opinion of their subjugated citizenry. The North Vietnamese understood clearly the weaknesses of America's relative restraint, its defensive stance, and its increasing domestic anti-war movement. They exploited these advantages to the full, guided by one principle: winning.

One of their prime strategic advantages lay in their use of Cambodia. Cambodia, headed by the effective quisling King Sihanouk, officially adopted a stance of neutrality. This neutrality represented a sham, however, since Sihanouk permitted the North Vietnamese Army (NVA) and the Viet Cong (VC) to operate on Cambodian territory. He did so out of fear of North Vietnam and in the hope that the North Vietnamese would not attack him while he attempted to deal with the Khmer Rouge.

The NVA and Viet Cong used this favorable situation to create numerous bases just across the Cambodian border from South Vietnam, enabling them to launch attacks and then retreat to their "neutral" refuge where the U.S. usually refused to authorize its troops to follow them. As U.S. Secretary of State Henry Kissinger said, "Washington had convinced itself that the four Indochinese states were separate entities, even though the communists had been treating them as a single theater for two decades and were conducting a coordinated strategy with respects to all of them." (Shaw, 2005, 3).

Furthermore, the North Vietnamese developed a shortened supply route through Cambodia to lessen dependence on the partially compromised Ho Chi Minh Trail traversing Laos. Sihanouk allowed Hanoi to use the deep water port of Sihanoukville to bring weaponry and supplies in from ships sailing out of communist China, from where the Viet Cong moved them the short distance to the South Vietnamese border, along the so-called Sihanoukville Trail, without fear of American interdiction.

Many historians point to the American bombing of Cambodia in an attempt to cripple Vietnamese supply lines as one of the primary reasons the Khmer Rouge was able to recruit so many members and gain the support of Cambodians. From 1965-1973, the United States routinely dropped bombs in Eastern Cambodia, which was also the region the Khmer Rouge established its first insurgent base in. Rural Cambodians in these communities developed extremely hostile views towards the Americans, giving the Khmer Rouge an opportunity to mobilize that anger and instill a sense of Cambodian nationalism.

At the same time, it can also be argued that the American bombing of Cambodia served to cripple the Khmer Rouge. Regardless of the intention, American bombings prevented the Khmer Rouge from toppling the Lon Nol regime and capturing Phnom Penh in 1970 and 1973, and without the devastating impact of those bombings, the Khmer Rouge may have come to power earlier than 1975, ultimately resulting in an even greater genocide.

In a similar way, albeit on a slightly more modest scale, the Cambodian Campaign placed the Americans suddenly in a temporary position of martial dominance. They had destroyed the logistical basis for North Vietnamese military operations in South Vietnam for at least a year and possibly longer. Had this been used as a springboard for further offensives in Cambodia and Laos, the strong possibility exists the U.S. Army could have eliminated any chance of a communist victory in the South, even without invading North Vietnam proper. But once again, politics intervened, and the Americans, casting away the successes of the Cambodian Campaign, continued with the status quo until the war ended with the Viet Cong uniting Vietnam as one country.

In the immediate aftermath, the Khmer Rouge would take power over all of Cambodia by 1975, and the leaders of communist Vietnam would go on to admit that they played a definitive role in establishing the Khmer Rouge, even though they ceased to support the regime following 1973. At that point, China took over arming and training members of the regime.

The Khmer Rouge in Power

While the Khmer Rouge regime's ideological views were primarily shaped by Marxism and Leninism, the presence of fierce Cambodian nationalism and overwhelming xenophobia made it unique when compared to other communist regimes.

A focus on Cambodia's history as an independent nation, particularly the glorification of the Khmer Empire, which ruled from 802-1431 in the region, greatly influenced the approach the Khmer Rouge took to ruling. Aside from that empire and its remnants, most notably Angkor War, the strength of Cambodia as an independent state was not consistent, with Thai, Vietnamese, and French forces exerting control over the population for various periods of time. Given that background, locals looked to the Khmer Empire's reign as the last time Cambodia was truly free of outside interference.

In the eyes of the Khmer Rouge, returning to a pure Cambodian state required putting Cambodia first, and the regime subsequently adopted extremely xenophobic views towards the Chinese and Vietnamese. Anti-Vietnamese sentiments were exacerbated by the Vietnam War, which many saw as a conflict Cambodia had no stake in that nevertheless spilled into their territory. As a result, the Khmer Rouge aimed to eliminate individuals of Chinese and Vietnamese descent, including those who were partially Khmer. Even members of the leadership in the Khmer Rouge who had mixed backgrounds were eliminated or adopted similar views, renouncing their heritage and advocating for ethnic cleansing.

Socially, the Khmer Rouge hoped to create a classless, agrarian society with a self-reliant economy. Pol Pot was the major proponent of this ideology, having been impressed by the tribes of rural Cambodia whom he had spent time among. He believed that their sustenance-based lifestyle was a form of early and natural communism, making it the purest form of society possible. To some extent, members of those rural communities were respected for having turned to communist ideals prior to the rise of communism, and, in turn, they received less harsh treatment than individuals from urban backgrounds.

Pol Pot also believed many communist regimes took unnecessary steps to slowly transition to a fully communist society. As a result of this view, he adopted a policy of abrupt change for the regime. For instance, cities were evacuated almost immediately, Cambodians were stripped of their individuality, all property was seized, and all citizens entered agricultural and labor camps to support the country's economy.

Prior to the Khmer Rouge taking power, Cambodia was an overwhelmingly Buddhist nation, but Pol Pot headed an atheist regime and immediately outlawed all religious expression in Cambodia. The primary religions affected were Buddhism, Christianity, and Islam, with Buddhists and Muslims taking the brunt of the abuse. During the regime's rule, the sole Catholic cathedral in Phnom Penh was burned, roughly 25,000 Buddhist monks were executed along with

Christians and Muslim clergy, and Muslims were forced to eat pork. Despite these efforts, the influence of Buddhism remained strong throughout Cambodia thanks to its longstanding history in the country and its popularity among individuals of all social classes.

In addition to stark social changes that would last four years, residents of Cambodia experienced torture, murder, starvation, and other atrocities at the hands of the Khmer Rouge. Historians still debate how much the Khmer Rouge's leaders knew about the regime's crimes as they were going on, but the impact of the regime on civilian life was clear.

The first step the Khmer Rouge regime took was to completely isolate Cambodia from foreign influences, in line with their xenophobic ideology. The regime went on to close every school, hospital, and factory, and they also abolished beacons of capitalism such as the banking industry, financial firms, and currency. The ultimate goal of these initial changes was to not only ensure subservience, but to quickly craft a society and future generations that were solely focused on agrarian life, lacking the education and means to pursue high level or individualistic endeavors.

Upon evacuating major cities such as Phnom Penh in order to relocate urban citizens to the collectivist communities, the Khmer Rouge told residents that they were briefly being moved out of the city due to the threat of the United States bombing Cambodia's major cities. Any individual who resisted evacuation would watch their house be burned by Khmer Rouge forces prior to being executed for failing to obey the regime's direct orders. The Khmer Rouge would go on to seize all belongings in people's homes and all their personal possessions, claiming that the regime needed it for the common good.

After being taken from their homes, citizens were sent on seemingly endless marches to rural areas, with children, the elderly, and the ill dying in the thousands as a result of the forced marches. These evacuations were not unprecedented in Cambodia, as the Khmer Rouge had performed small-scale evacuations in the early 1970s, but the 1975 relocation of citizens was the first widespread effort, as well as the first to tackle central urban areas.

These forced relocations served the purpose of providing the Khmer Rouge regime with an agricultural workforce who could meet the nation's sustenance needs, allowing their forces to continue defending the regime's interests. At the same time, it also served the purpose of eliminating social and economic classes, and since urban populations tended to be wealthier than rural populations, eliminating the cities and forcing all citizens to work in agriculture would create what the Khmer Rouge viewed as an even playing field.

While rice production prior to the regime's rule was roughly one ton per hectare of land, the Khmer Rouge expected its forced laborers to produce three tons of rice per hectare of land. Workers were expected to work 12 hours each day with no breaks for food or rest.

Ultimately, those who had lived in urban areas lacked agricultural skills, resulting in widespread famine when quotas were not met and the land was overused. Furthermore, if an individual gathered wild fruits or vegetables, they could be executed because it was considered a form of a capitalism that detracted from the equality the Khmer Rouge hoped to create.

As a result of famine and poor working conditions, large numbers of individuals died from sheer exhaustion, illness, and starvation. With the Khmer Rouge eschewing Western ideals and technology, many died due to lack of access to medical supplies that could have addressed treatable ailments.

Aside from forced labor, the Khmer Rouge implemented a variety of policies that further marginalized residents of Cambodia. For instance, commercial fishing was outlawed in 1976 because it was considered a form of personal enterprise, eliminating a source of food that roughly 80% of Cambodians depended on as their sole source of protein.

The regime outlawed the use of currency and burned educational materials and books, which they viewed as outside influences on Cambodia. Education was considered unnecessary for a sustenance-based, agrarian society. In line with this thinking, businessmen, educators, and anyone considered highly educated became victims of genocide in the Khmer Rouge's notorious killing fields. Even the perception of intellectualism was considered grounds for execution, meaning something as simple as wearing glasses could result in death as it suggested you spent time reading novels and research studies. Throughout this process, Cambodia's entire social structure suffered an upheaval and was ultimately destroyed, leaving no economic or social apparatus to fall back on after the end of the regime.

Alongside the forced labor and famine of the Cambodians, the regime went about executing an untold number of dissidents, both real and imagined. Anyone the regime believed was a political enemy, a spy for a foreign nation, or educated and connected enough to work towards the upheaval of the regime was promptly executed. This included all intellectuals and could branch out to uneducated people who had soft hands, as soft hands suggested a lack of manual labor and therefore the potential of being educated and versed in politics. Disobedience also resulted in execution, with infractions including escape attempts, unauthorized eating, and displays of individual identity over collectivist ideals.

Lastly, mere social status and attitudes could result in execution or torture under the Khmer Rouge regime. Openly religious individuals, particularly Buddhist monks and Cham Muslims, were executed since religion was viewed as contrary to Cambodian ideals. It was believed by the Khmer Rouge that individuals should put all of their faith in the regime and the Cambodian nation to ensure a peaceful and classless society. Individuals who were part of a family considered illegitimate by the Khmer Rouge (perhaps as a result of marriages between different ethnicities) were at risk of execution, and those who were separated from their families would face execution if they attempted to interact with them. In the same vein, familial bonds were disregarded since the regime insisted each person's highest commitment should be to the state, meaning that families were split and only allowed minimal interaction under the threat of execution.

The concept of personal privacy was also eliminated, with anyone who attempted to lead an individual lifestyle being banned. Thus, sexual activity was punishable by death, travel was forbidden, eating and sleeping in private spaces were taboo, and personal utensils, clothes, and tools were outlawed.

Like many languages in the Indochinese family, the Khmer language, which is indigenous to Cambodia, has a complicated method of defining the social standing of both the speaker and the person being spoken to. This is enshrined in the language and a common part of speaking. However, these innate linguistic characteristics ran contrary to the Khmer Rouge's desire for a classless society. As such, they were all outlawed, and in place of traditional identifiers, Cambodians were encouraged to solely refer to others as their friends or comrades, in addition to avoiding the use of bowing and respectful, clasped hand gestures.

The Khmer Rouge also went on to introduce new vocabulary to the language, all of which was designed to place a greater importance on simplicity, agrarian life, and lack of individualism. The regime established a new word for creating a new sense of character and created the concept of individuals serving as parts of the greater machine of Angkar, or the ruling party. Labeling the ruling body Angkar also served a clear purpose, as it tied the regime to the old Khmer Empire linguistically. The concept of nostalgia was also introduced in the language, but with the negative connotation of an illness, as speaking favorable of the past was grounds for execution. Lastly, rural forms of words such as mother and father were favored over their urban counterparts, emphasizing that rural life was the truer version of being Cambodian.

In all, the Khmer Rouge established more than 150 prisons for their perceived enemies, with Tuol Sleng in central Phnom Penh becoming the most infamous. Roughly 20,000 inmates were housed in Tuol Sleng over the course of its four years of operation, and only 7 survived their imprisonment. The Khmer Rouge implemented a variety of inhumane torture methods, and some of the equipment remains at the site of Tuol Sleng prison, which is now the Tuol Sleng Genocide Museum. Torture operations were led by Khang Khek Ieu, often referred to as Duch. Ieu is the only member of the Khmer Rouge leadership to receive a criminal sentence prior to passing away.

Along with the prisons, the Khmer Rouge established countless killing fields across the country of Cambodia. Prisoners would be taken there from their respective prisons or individuals would be brought to the fields directly from their homes or the collectivist camps. The executions were carried out using sharp leaves to slit the throats of the victims, while infants and young children were routinely slammed against trees. The Khmer Rouge adopted a policy of punishing an entire family for one family member's perceived wrongdoing, operating under the assumption that children may avenge their parents. As a result, the regime determined it was best to kill an entire family and eliminate the potential for future retaliation.

Research suggests that there are nearly 20,000 mass graves dating from 1975-1979 across the entirety of Cambodia, and estimates of the death count range from 740,000-3,000,000. Yale University puts the number at 1.7 million victims, while various United Nations agencies place the toll at 2-3 million. The most commonly accepted death count is between 1.4-2.2 million, which would represent roughly 25% of the country's population. Researchers believe 50% of the deaths were the result of executions and the other half came about from overworking, starvation, and illness. Furthermore, an estimated 300,000 people died in the year following the Khmer Rouge's fall as a result of the effects of the regime's actions on agriculture and food access.

A Cambodian war tribunal, backed by the United Nations, found the Khmer Rouge guilty of a wide variety of crimes against humanity. Pol Pot died prior to being arrested, and other top Khmer Rouge leaders died while in custody. Duch, the sole member of the Khmer Rouge leadership to have received a sentence, is still serving life in prison. Two other top leaders are currently undergoing trials but are expected to pass away prior to a verdict being reached.

Michael Darter's picture of a killing field at Choeung Ek

The End of the Khmer Rouge

Pol Pot feared that Vietnamese intervention could topple his regime, and in 1978, he anticipated that Vietnam would send troops into Cambodia to liberate its people from the regime. In response, he sent troops into Vietnam to preemptively eliminate that potential interference.

These Khmer Rouge troops predominantly stayed on the border, looting villages and massacring residents. The most notorious of these massacres occurred in the village of Ba Chuc, where only two of the 3,157 residents survived the Khmer Rouge's invasion.

Ultimately, Vietnam's troops pushed the Khmer Rouge forces back into Cambodia, and perhaps not surprisingly, tensions between Vietnam and the Khmer Rouge only worsened. Refugees continued to pour into Vietnam, border disputes were ongoing, and the brutality of the Khmer Rouge was fresh on Vietnamese minds. Finally, the Vietnamese sent troops into Cambodia to topple the Khmer Rouge in December 1978, and they were backed by the Kampuchean United Front for National Salvation, which consisted of former Khmer Rouge members who had defected. Together, these troops entered Cambodia and captured Phnom Penh in January 1979.

While Cambodians had longstanding fears of foreign powers intervening in their government, particularly as a result of Vietnamese and Thai influences on the nation, individuals who defected from the Khmer Rouge took up arms alongside Vietnam's forces. After having sided with Vietnam, the former Khmer Rouge members were declared the leaders of the People's Republic of Kampuchea. They were the ones who ultimately toppled the Khmer Rouge and restored order to the country, even as both the Khmer Rouge and China labeled them a Vietnamese puppet government in an attempt to negate their legitimacy.

After the regime had officially been toppled and a new government was in place, the Khmer Rouge's leaders did not give up hope. For the next decade, the Khmer Rouge would exert power over portions of Cambodia close to the Thai border, where its leaders successfully hid to avoid persecution. These regions were predominantly mountainous, rural communities mirroring the northeastern villages the regime had initially garnered support from in the 1960s. However, these strongholds were not self-reliant, primarily relying on diamond and timber smuggling, in addition to Chinese military and resource support, to maintain operations.

In spite of the Cambodian Genocide and the political and military defeat of the Khmer Rouge, the regime maintained a seat at the United Nations, held by Thiounn Prasith, who was a contemporary of Pol Pot and Ieng Sary in the Paris Student Group and an attendee of the Kampuchea People's Revolutionary Party Second Congress. Prasith officially represented Democratic Kampuchea through 1982 and then represented the newly formed Coalition Government of Democratic Kampuchea in later years, both of which were backed by former members of the Khmer Rouge.

The United Nations voted in favor of the Khmer Rouge holding its seat under the name of the Coalition Government of Democratic Kampuchea in 1982. Western nations argued that it was a more valid government representation, as the government established in Cambodia following the collapse of the Khmer Rouge was, in essence, a Vietnamese government. In 1988, Margaret Thatcher voiced acceptance of the Khmer Rouge playing a role in the future governing of

Cambodia, whereas Sweden, on the other hand, dropped support for the Khmer Rouge after years of favorable votes after becoming aware of the regime's atrocities. Ultimately, the Khmer Rouge would hold the seat in the United Nations until 1991.

The Vietnamese invasion of Cambodia to topple the Khmer Rouge was supported by the Soviet Union, and in the years to come, it would have a serious impact on the political landscape of Cambodia, as well as Southeast Asia as a whole. In response to the invasion of Cambodia, China invaded North Vietnam in retaliation, but after China retreated, both sides claimed victory. China and the United States would go on to support the formation of the Coalition Government of Democratic Kampuchea, which functioned as a government-in-exile and consisted of former Khmer Rouge members and former royalists. This government existed in opposition to the Vietnamese puppet government based in Phnom Penh.

By 1980, both East and Central Cambodia were controlled by the Vietnamese and their Cambodian counterparts, but West Cambodia remained disputed and fighting continued between rebel forces and the Vietnamese. Throughout this time, rebel forces planted land mines in rural communities to combat the Vietnamese, and many of these mines never exploded and are still active today, maiming and killing civilians.

Of all of the rebel forces, the Khmer Rouge remained the most visible and the most supported. The rebel forces were backed by China, the United Kingdom, the United States, and Thailand, with the United Kingdom and the United States solely supporting rebel factions not associated with the Khmer Rouge.

Following the fall of the Khmer Rouge, the former regime's leaders struggled to maintain momentum. They established the Patriotic and Democratic Front of the Great National Union of Kampuchea in 1979, and in 1981, they officially denounced their ties to communism, instead emphasizing the importance of Cambodian nationalism and rejecting the influence of Vietnam. This, while appearing to be a major shift, meant very little, as the Khmer Rouge had consistently based its ideology in nationalism and xenophobia, meaning an official turn away from communism affected little in practice. The Khmer Rouge regime did not mirror other communism movements, and as a result its ties or lack thereof to the broader communist fight were insignificant. Most likely, this was to separate the regime from the Vietnamese communists who had toppled their control.

Pol Pot officially resigned as the leader of the Khmer Rouge in 1985, with Khieu Samphan taking his place as the head of the regime. However, Pol Pot remained the figurehead of the Khmer Rouge and the motivating factor behind its recruitment efforts, message, and ideology. He routinely gave speeches, appearing to be extremely charismatic and interested in the continued existence of an independent Cambodian state.

While many foreigners were appalled by the actions of the Khmer Rouge, as well as many Cambodians, there seemed to be a significant faction of Cambodians who truly supported Pol Pot due to his charisma and message of fierce nationalism. Of course, it'd be hard to say how many approved of him as a leader as opposed to his message, since there continued to be widespread hatred of the Vietnamese.

Vietnam eventually offered to leave Cambodia, allowing a truly representative government to take the place of Phnom Penh's puppet government, but the Vietnamese stipulated that any future government must prohibit former members of the Khmer Rouge from holding leadership positions entirely. The rebel forces, backed by China and the United States, argued against this, and despite an agreement never being made, the Vietnamese began to withdraw from Cambodia in 1985 and did so completely by 1989. This gave their puppet government the time it needed to build a strong enough state apparatus to fend off the attempts of rebel forces to exact power over Cambodia.

Following this, the government established by Vietnam signed an agreement with the rebel forces in 1991 that set the ground for national elections and the disarmament of both sides of the conflict. Nevertheless, the Khmer Rouge began armed fighting once again in 1992, ultimately boycotting the election and rejecting its results in 1993. The newly formed government after the elections consisted of the former Vietnam-supported leaders, as well as rebel royalists and communists no longer associated with the Khmer Rouge. In response to this government, the Khmer Rouge created the Provisional Government of National Union and National Salvation of Cambodia in July 1994.

In 1996, roughly 50% of Khmer Rouge militants left the former regime in an act of mass defection, and as a result, the Khmer Rouge found itself willing work with the newly formed government when a royalist, Prince Rannaridh, reached out to Khmer Rouge leaders for support. Prince Rannaridh, however, refused to interact with Pol Pot, and this refusal resulted in the Khmer Rouge leadership dividing into factions and warring amongst themselves for roughly a year. The impasse ended with Pol Pot being imprisoned by the Khmer Rouge itself until his death in April of 1998.

In the months to come, the Khmer Rouge would apologize for its actions in the 1970s, with the vast majority of its former leaders surrendering to authorities by 1999. At that point, the Khmer Rouge ceased to exist.

The negative impact of the Khmer Rouge is not debatable. However, the intentions and motives of its leaders continue to be contested. Furthermore, there has been significant discussion as to how to appropriately pursue justice in international courts. In many ways, these views have remained unchanged, but in others they have overwhelmingly shifted.

Despite the fact the Khmer Rouge was in power just 40 years ago, the regime's commitment to closing Cambodia's borders and limiting foreign awareness proved effective enough to prevent the creation of a comprehensive historical record. In fact, most histories regarding the Khmer Rouge are limited to a handful of authors, most of whom aimed to support particular viewpoints or political agendas.

Historical evidence that paints the Khmer Rouge regime in a negative light tends to be come from contemporary Cambodians who witnessed and suffered through the Cambodian Genocide, highlighting the regime's disastrous impact on civilian life. However, these accounts are necessarily one-sided, and they can't fully answer the intentions, motives, and theoretical internal justifications of the regime at the time.

Alternatively, histories that depict the Khmer Rouge in a positive light often depend on historical data, statements, and other documents that were created by the regime itself. Given that a genocidal regime would not want outsiders to become aware of its actions, it goes without saying that many of these resources hid the regime's agenda and true impact. In fact, Khmer Rouge documents imply that there was no unnecessary brutality at all.

All things considered, it's safe to assume that historical accounts of the Khmer Rouge will continue to be limited based on the different viewpoints of authors and limited access to accurate historical documents.

Online Resources

Other books about the Khmer on Amazon

Further Reading

Bartrop P, "Pol Pot," A Biographical Encyclopedia of Contemporary Genocide: Portraits of Evil and Good (ABC-CLIO, 2012).

Becker E, "The Birth of Modern Cambodia," When the War Was Over: Cambodia and the Khmer Rouge Revolution (Public Affairs, 1998).

Becker E; Khieu Ponnary, 83, First Wife of Pol Pot, Cambodian Despot (New York: New York Times, 2003).

Bultmann D, "Inside Cambodian Insurgency," A Sociological Perspective on Civil wars and Conflict (Ashgate 2015)

Chandler D, Brother Number One: A Political Biography of Pol Pot (Colorado: Westview Press, 1999).

Chandler D, "Cambodia 1884-1975," The Emergency of Modern Southeast Asia (Hawaii: University of Hawaii Press, 2005).

Chandler D, A History of Cambodia (Colorado: Westview Press, 2008).

Chandler D, "Legacies of World War II in Indochina," in Legacies of World War II in South and East Asia, ed. David Koh Wee Hock, (Singapore: Institute of Southeast Asian Studies, 2007): 23-4.

Chandler D, The Tragedy of Cambodian History: Politics, War, and Revolution since 1945 (New Haven: Yale University Press, 1991).

"Confession of Hu Nim," The Confession of Hu Nim, aka Phoas (Documentation Center of Cambodia, 1975).

Cook S & Mosyakov D, Genocide in Cambodia and Rwanda: New Perspectives (Routledge, 2017).

Fletcher D, The Khmer Rouge (New York City: Time, 2009).

Frey R, Genocide and International Justice (Infobase Publishing, 2009).

Garrett C, "In Search of Grandeur: France and Vietnam 1940-1946," The Review of Politics 29, no. 3 (July 1967).

Johnman A; "The Case of Cambodia;" Contemporary Genocides: Causes, Cases, Consequences (Programma Interdisciplinair Onderzoek naar Oorzaken van Mensenrechtenschendingen, 1996).

Khamboly D, Khmer Rouge History (Cambodia Tribunal Monitor 2013).

Khmer Rouge History (Cambodia Tribunal Monitor).

Kiernan B, "The American Bombardment of Kampuchea 1969-1973," Vietnam Generation (1989).

Kiernan B, "The Cambodian Genocide 1975-1979," in A Century of Genocide: Critical Essays and Eyewitness Accounts, ed. Samuel Trotten and William S. Parsons, 283-313 (New York: Routledge, 2009).

Kiernan B; "The Changing of the Vanguard;" How Pol Pot Came to Power: Colonialism, Nationalism, and Communism in Cambodia, 1930-1975 (Yale University Press; 2004).

Kiernan B; The Pol Pot Regime: Race, Power, and Genocide in Cambodia Under the Khmer Rouge, 1975-1979 (London: Yale University Press; 1997).

Lind M, Vietnam: The Necessary War: A Reinterpretation of America's Most Disastrous Military Conflict (Free Press, 1999).

Linter B, Dining with the Dear Leader (Phnom Penh: Asia Times, 2007).

Locard H, "State Violence in Democratic Kampuchea (1975-1979) and Retribution   (1979-2004)," European Review of History 12, no. 1 (Spring 2005).

Luftglass S, "Crossroads in Cambodia: The United Nation's Responsibility to Withdraw Involvement from the Establishment of a Cambodian Tribunal to Prosecute the Khmer Rouge," Virginia Law Review 90, no. 3 (2004).

Morris S, Vietnam and Cambodian Communism, (Cambodian Human Rights and Development Association, 2007).

Morris S, Why Vietnam Invaded Cambodia: Political Culture and the Causes of War (Stanford University Press, 1999).

Mosyakov D, "The Khmer Rouge and the Vietnamese Communists: A History of Their Relations as Told in the Soviet Archives," Genocide in Cambodia and Rwanda (Yale Genocide Studies Program, 2004).

Owen N, The Emergence of Modern Southeast Asia: A New History (Honolulu: University of Hawaii Press, 2005).

Raszelenberg P, "The Khmers Rouges and the Final Solution," History and Memory (1999).

Rowley K, Second Life, Second Death: The Khmer Rouge After 1978 (2007).

Sharp B, Counting Hell: The Death Toll of the Khmer Rouge Regime in Cambodia (2005).

Shawcross W; Sideshow: Kissing, Nixon, and the Destruction of Cambodia (Cooper Square, 2002).

Short P, "Initiation to the Maquis," Pol Pot: Anatomy of a Nightmare (Macmillan, 2007).

Steinberg D, et al., In Search of Southeast Asia: A Modern History (Hawaii: University of Hawaii Press, 1987).

Sutsakhan S, The Khmer Republic at War and the Final Collapse (Washington DC: United States Army Center of Military History, 1987).

Thayer N, Cambodia: Misperceptions and Peace (Washington Quarterly, 1991)

Tolson M, Dam the Fish (Ratanakira Province, Cambodia: Inter Press Service, 2013).

Tyner, J, The Killing of Cambodia: Geography, Genocide and the Unmaking of Space (Ashgate Publishing, 2008).

Ung S, I Survived the Killing Fields: The True Life Story of a Cambodian Refugee (2011).

Vickery M, Cambodia: 1975-1982 (Boston: South End Press, 1984)

Weitz E, "Racial Communism: Cambodia Under the Khmer Rouge," A Century of Genocide: Utopias of Race and Nation (New Jersey: Princeton University Press, 2005).

Wessinger C; Millennialism, Persecution, and Violence: Historical Cases (Syracuse University Press; 2000)

Yimsut R, "Forward," Facing the Khmer Rouge: A Cambodian Journey (Rutgers University Press, 2011).

Young L, Cambodian Political History: Former PM Pen Sovann's Left Perspective — Hostile to the Khmer Rouge and the Present Rulers (Montreal: Centre for Research on Globalization, 2013).

Free Books by Charles River Editors

We have brand new titles available for free most days of the week. To see which of our titles are currently free, click on this link.

Discounted Books by Charles River Editors

We have titles at a discount price of just 99 cents everyday. To see which of our titles are currently 99 cents, click on this link.

Printed in Great Britain
by Amazon